Especially for: _____

From: _____

_____

four paws from heaven

M.R. Wells, Kris Young, and Connie Fleishauer

rachaelhale

HARVEST HOUSE PUBLISHERS

EUGENE OREGON

Four Paws from Heaven—*Gift Edition*

© Dissero Brands Limited (New Zealand) 2007.
All worldwide rights reserved.
www.rachaelhale.com

Text Copyright © 2008 by M.R. Wells, Kris Young, and Connie Fleishauer

Published by Harvest House Publishers
Eugene, Oregon 97402
www.harvesthousepublishers.com

ISBN-13: 978-0-7369-2203-6
ISBN-10: 0-7369-2203-2

Design and production by Garborg Design Works, Savage, Minnesota

Harvest House Publishers has made every effort to trace the ownership of all poems and quotes. In the event of a question arising from the use of a poem or quote, we regret any error made and will be pleased to make the necessary correction in future editions of this book.

Scripture quotations are taken from the HOLY BIBLE, NEW INTERNATIONAL VERSION®. NIV®. Copyright©1973, 1978, 1984 by the International Bible Society. Used by permission of Zondervan. All rights reserved.

Printed in China

08 09 10 11 12 13 14 15 / LP / 10 9 8 7 6 5 4 3 2 1

doggie insight
Introductory Paws

Man's best friends aren't likely to launch into human speech, but we believe God uses them nonetheless in the way the book of Romans describes: "For since the creation of the world God's invisible qualities—his eternal power and divine nature—have been clearly seen, being understood from what has been made, so that men are without excuse" (Romans 1:20). Today, dogs play a vital role in many of our lives. They're often treated as part of the family. People connect powerfully with tales about these treasured pets. Even if God hasn't opened their mouths, we believe He can use them to speak to our hearts and build a bridge to deeper spiritual insights.

Beauty comes from within.
<small>PROVERB</small>

gracie looks at the heart
God Sees Who We Are Inside

Have you ever considered the difference between how you see yourself, how your dog sees you, and how God sees you? I have, and I've found it quite revealing. Viewing myself through Gracie's eyes has reminded me of God's perspective… which doesn't always match up with my own.

Gracie didn't seem to see what I saw in the mirror. Even on my bad mornings, unless she was sick, she'd bound up to

me, tail wagging so furiously it seemed she was about to take off and fly. Never once did she appear to look down on me for my unkempt, ugly, unseemly, less-than-movie-star appearance.

It amazes me how God used Gracie to teach me this basic truth—that what makes me lovable and worthy isn't my external body that decays with each tick of the clock. My self-worth shouldn't be measured by the amount of love and approval I receive from other people based on how they rate the accessories and accoutrements adorning my outer man. No, it is my heart, the internal, eternal part of me, that defines who I am.

God sees that…and so do our dogs.

Viewing myself through Gracie's eyes has reminded me of God's perspective.

He who loves God above all things is at length the friend of God.
GOTTFRIED LEIBNITZ

first loves
Hang On to Your First Love

Stuart loved to race through the house as a pup. He'd dash off across the living room, through the kitchen and den, and back into the living room once more. Then he would leap on and off the sofa and begin all over again, running the same route at top speed. This special puppy behavior of Stuart's brought us much entertainment and laughter.

Stuart's older now, but from time to time he still runs a repeat path the way he used to. It delights us to see that he hasn't entirely lost this behavior he treasured so much in his youth.

It probably delights God when we revive the enthusiasm we had when we first came to love Him.

who's afraid of the big bad dog?

Fear God, Not Man

Make God thy Friend, and then it's no matter who is thy Enemy.

THOMAS FULLER

Huxley loved chasing cats because he knew they hated it. He knew they would run from him. He knew they were all afraid of the big bad dog. But there was one tiny kitten, Wally, who did not succumb to Huxley's torment.

Wally was a runt, but he didn't seem aware of how tiny he was. Or maybe he just didn't believe Huxley was the big bad enemy. Whatever the cause, Wally chose to approach instead of run.

Wally marched right over and lowered his head into Huxley's

food bowl, and then he looked up at its owner. Huxley eyed the intruder in apparent disbelief. This kitten should have been terrified.

But Wally overcame fear…and Huxley must have sensed that his scare tactics wouldn't work on this cat. They soon became friends. Huxley let Wally share his food and take naps on his back. The two remained pals 'til the day Wally died.

I have found that facing fear the way Wally did is the best way to fight it. Sometimes the worst enemy is fear itself. Victory comes when I seek the Lord and ask Him to cover me and guard me and guide me through.

Wally was a runt, but he didn't seem aware of how tiny he was. Or maybe he just didn't believe Huxley was the big bad enemy.

divine dog tags
Discovering Our True Identity

O Lord, you have searched me and you know me.

PSALM 139:1

Max was a Boston terrier. Some folks thought he was ugly, but we thought otherwise. Max's eyes were wide apart and bugged out. When he stared straight ahead, people on both sides thought he was looking at them.

Ugly or not, Max's identity didn't come mainly from his looks. It came from his unique personality and from being ours. Everyone in our area knew who Max was and that he was owned by the Fleishauers. Occasionally, he got lost, but someone always brought him back. He wore dog tags, but they weren't really needed. He belonged to us and we belonged to him. No questions asked!

It's the same with God. No matter how much I've changed through the years, I am God's child, and He knows and loves me—no dog tags needed.

a bucket of trust
God Will Meet Your Needs

All I have seen teaches me to trust the Creator for all I have not seen.
RALPH WALDO EMERSON

Mealtime was the highlight of Gracie's day. The dog loved to eat. When I went out to feed her each morning, she became so excited her tail wagged her whole body. But her look of delirious joy wasn't based on the level of dry food stored in our five-gallon plastic bucket. Gracie had no idea that sometimes it was filled to the brim, while other times it was nearly empty. I never caught her, in a secret moment, cleverly using her paws to lift

the lid and peek inside. Nor would she have dreamed of writing "dog food" on our shopping list…even if she could.

Gracie didn't look to the bucket or the store for her needs…she looked to me. She wasn't anxious about her provision because she knew I loved her and would take care of her. She trusted me with all her heart.

It's dawned on me that I, too, have Someone who loves and cares for me. He has even promised, in writing, to supply all my needs. I've lost countless anxious hours staring down at the bucket…hours God meant for peace if I'd only gazed up at the bucket-Filler instead.

She wasn't anxious about her provision because she knew I loved her and would take care of her.

the purpose-driven dog
When It's God's Will, There's a Way

Every path hath a puddle.

JOHN RAY

Max was a small and somewhat timid dog, but once he realized he was part of our family, he became our watchdog and protector. He would actually scare people off with his loud bark and mean growl.

Once I opened the door to a man who seemed suspicious. His eyes roamed the house as we talked. I was uncertain about what to do. Max took over, baring his teeth and growling till the man decided to leave. Max knew his purpose in life: to keep the Fleishauers safe.

Max didn't let size or timidity keep him from serving his family. God has a purpose for each of us. If it's His will, He'll provide a way if we will just obey, step out, and trust in Him.

wait!

God's Timing Is Perfect

*Set not your Loaf in,
'til the Oven's hot.*

THOMAS FULLER

After I had opened my heart and home to my two dogs, I hired a trainer to teach me how to teach them. One command he urged me to use was the "wait" command, to halt them behind boundaries. He said they must not cross the line without permission, whether it was the threshold of a room or the curb between sidewalk and street. Someday, he said, this might save their lives.

I soon saw what he meant.

I started walking Morgan and Biscuit around my neighborhood. My eager beaver canines did not always stop at corners. Now and then they would leap off the curb. Though they were on a leash, they had just enough rope to put themselves at risk. I told them to "sit" when we came to a

corner. After glancing both ways, I'd say "let's go" and we'd cross the street together.

Of course, the dogs didn't realize their danger, but they had learned to trust and obey me, so they did what I asked.

Sometimes we must trust and obey a "wait" command we are given that we don't understand. I love Morgan and Biscuit and want to keep them from harm. My Father loves me infinitely more. I can trust His "wait," knowing it is for my good and that His timing is always perfect.

One command he urged me to use was the "wait" command, to halt them behind boundaries.

more than he could chew
To Hoard Is Human; to Share, Divine

Much would have more.

JOHN CLARKE

Morgan loved treats. A frequent scenario went like this. Biscuit mouthed a bone and settled down to chew. Morgan saw and snatched her prize away. Biscuit trotted off and grabbed a second bone to gnaw. Morgan dropped his bone and yanked away her new one. She went for the bone he had abandoned...and on it went. Morgan's mission was keeping both bones for himself.

Trouble was, he could only chew one bone at a time.

I've realized that I, too, often grab more bones than I can chew. Piling up more bones won't help me any more than it helped Morgan. But God says there's one thing I can store up to my heart's content. That's spiritual treasure—and one way I can gain it is by giving of my bones.

if a dog could eat forever
Our Appetites Can Get Us into Trouble

Greed oft o'erreaches itself.

AESOP

For most of her life, Gracie ate like a vacuum cleaner—sucking food in so fast she barely had time to chew. She'd lick her bowl for every trace, down to the dust particles. Then she'd look up at me, hoping beyond hope that I'd give her another scoop. Maybe two or three times a year I'd let her have a few more morsels.

Occasionally, as I watched her inhale her food as if she were in

She'd lick her bowl for every trace, down to the dust particles. Then she'd look up at me, hoping beyond hope that I'd give her another scoop.

a kibble-eating contest, I wondered what would happen if I dumped the whole 20-pound bag of dog food into a bucket and let her eat as much as she wanted. Would she chow down until she passed out? Would she gobble and gobble until she ballooned into a freaky 500-pound sumo dog?

I never tried this experiment. As her owner, I chose to set the limits of her food intake: not too little, lest she starve, and not too much, lest she become obese. I hope she realized that as she looked at me with those big, begging eyes of hers. *Please, give me MORE!*

Too often, I look at God like that. But perhaps God sees it differently. Perhaps He knows that I don't need more—I just need more of Him.

Love doesn't make the world go 'round.
Love makes the ride worthwhile.

FRANKLIN P. JONES